Passive Income - Beginners Guide

Proven Business Models and Strategies to Become Financially Free and Make an Additional $10,000 a Month

Joel Jacobs

Table of Contents

Introduction

When you are working for someone else, they have control over your pay. Even if you have been working the same job for ten or more years, keeping this job is never guaranteed. The company you work for could get sold, go bankrupt, or decide to move locations, leaving you suddenly unemployed and without pay. What's worse, depending on the job market and your professional career, finding another job may not be quickly accomplished. For this reason, and among others, more and more people are turning to 'side hustles' to bring in a second income.

A passive income stream allows you to generate a line of income separate from your day job. "Passive income" refers to earnings that require little to no effort to earn or maintain—like a rental property or other enterprises where you do not have to be actively involved in operations. It gives you a little extra security and relief knowing that whatever happens with your 9 to 5, you won't have to worry about paying bills or putting food on the table. With a passive income stream, you can be as active or passive as you wish. You can put the work in once and then allow some money to trickle in for months and years later. Alternatively, you can maintain a profitable business that allows you the freedom to live the life you have always dreamed of.

This book is designed to simplify the process of getting started and maintaining a passive income. Whether you have a demanding career already or are staying home to raise your children, anyone can create a passive income. Learn how to generate more money each month to set aside for a rainy day, quit your day job, or put towards your future home. To truly have financial freedom, you need to have money coming from more than one source. Many of the ideas in this book require little or no upfront investment, so you don't have to wait until you save up enough to get started. You can use the information in this book today and benefit from starting now in just a few months. The process is not complex, and you can easily take advantage of multiple passive income streams so you won't have to worry about being financially strained again.

Chapter 1: Affiliate Marketing

Affiliate marketing has the potential to bring in 300 to 10,000 dollars a day. It is one of the most effective ways to start a passive income stream that can continuously grow for years. There are multiple ways to get started and platforms you can use to generate an affiliate marketing business. We start with this option because the information in this chapter can help you easily expand into other passive income opportunities.

What is Affiliate Marketing

Affiliate marketing is one of the most popular ways for anyone to make a steady income. You, the affiliate, find products you already enjoy using and promote them. Each time you contribute to a sale of the products, you make a commission. Products can be physical objects or services; there is also the potential to earn a small commission by promoting a company or brand. Commissions are tracked by using an affiliate link. There are a few ways to make a commission:

- Pay-per-sale — This is the standard method of earning for affiliate markers. With this approach, you earn a percentage of the sales when an individual clicks on your link. The person must purchase the product or service you are promoting to be compensated.
- Pay-per-lead — This method does not have to result in the sale of a product, but does involve the consumer performing a specific action. Pay-per-lead affiliates need to convince viewers to click on the link they provide and supply additional information for a company or brand. This typically gets viewers to sign up for a mailing list, subscribe to a social page, or download a digital product. You make a commission based on how many people complete the desired call to action.
- Pay-per-click — With pay-per-click affiliate marketing, you earn a percentage each time you drive traffic to a merchant's

website. The more web traffic you can redirect to the merchant's site, the more you can earn.

Affiliate Marketing Platforms

Blogging

Starting a blog is straightforward; you create content, hit publish, and do your best to get more readers every day. Blogs are an easy way to establish many affiliate links, as you can create different posts that review or promote multiple products. The key to being successful is to grow your reach organically. You want your content to rank high on Google search engines; this requires investing a bit more time learning proper search engine optimization.

How to get started:

1. First, decide what your blog will be about. Will it be a lifestyle blog, crafting corner, health and fitness-related, or other more specific topics. Choose something that you are familiar with and can continuously create content around.
2. Think of a catchy name for your blog. You want something short and memorable. You can include your name if you plan to create a brand around yourself, making it easier to sell products.
3. Once you have decided on a few name contenders, you need a hosting site —Bluehost, HostGator, GoDaddy. Most of these offer a free domain name with the hosting plan.
4. You need a blogging platform. WordPress is the most popular for bloggers, and you can set up ecommerce options.
5. Now, you are ready to customize your blog. You can use plenty of free themes with WordPress, or you can opt to buy a theme. Each can be customized to align with your own style.
6. After you are satisfied with the look, you need to get some content written. Many start with an introductory post that lets readers know what the blog is about, who they are, and what they can expect. You want to have a posting schedule and stick with it. If you say you will post two times a week, pick two days

to publish a new blog on those days. Readers are more likely to keep checking in with what you post when they can expect new content to take in. When writing your post, always end it with an open-ended question that will encourage readers to leave comments. This is important as it gets your content in higher rankings.

7. Create an email list generator. This will help you capture readers' information to let them know when you have a new post and other products that may interest them.

8. Once you have grown your audience, you can begin selling ad space on your blog. Also, consider other products or services that your audience wants to learn more about and are willing to pay for.

Podcasting

If writing content isn't your thing, but you have a knack for public speaking, podcasting might be your ticket into affiliate marketing. There are plenty of platforms that you can use to help set up your own podcast, but this option does require a little bit more of an investment in obtaining the right equipment. Like blogging, you will need a podcast hosting platform to publish content on. The following suggestions are great for beginners as they not only provide you with the right tools to get your podcast up and running, they are easy to use.

- Podbean
- BuzzSprout
- Blubrry Podcasting
- Transistor
- Smart Podcast Player
- Soundcloud

When choosing a hosting platform, you want to pay special attention to the file size and storage you are allotted. Podbean offers unlimited storage, and you can promote your podcast through various services. You still need a website and domain name to make it easier for the listener to find your content. Your website does not have to be complex. You can do this the same way you set up a blog, but will need to install the podcast WordPress plugin. Once you have this setup, you can begin recording your content.

The most important piece of equipment you will need to get started is a microphone. There are plenty of podcasting kits that come with a microphone and additional accessories that you will need, such as a shock mount to reduce noise and a mic arm for easy maneuvering while you are recording. You will also need a quality headset. You do not need to worry about investing in the best equipment, but you need to use a microphone that will lead to smooth recording. Do not use your camera's built-in microphone.

Now that you have the equipment, you can begin to plan your first episode. You want to have an outline of what you will be covering during that episode. To do this, you need to consider how long your episodes will be. There are no rules for the length of your podcast episodes need to be, your audience and content will be the determining factors. Some podcasts are under 10 minutes long; others record hour-long episodes that their audiences love.

Write a script to follow once you have an outline complete. This will help you better plan your episodes to account for pauses and will help you sound more professional. With your script, you are ready to record. To record, you will want podcast recording software that will allow you to record and edit your content. Audacity is free software that many podcast beginners use.

Consider what your intro and outro will be. If you are using music, you want to ensure that it is licensed-free. A few places to look for music include:

- Free Music Archive
- YouTube Audio Library
- Free Stock Music
- Envato Market
- SoundCloud

When you are satisfied with your first episode, you can upload it to your podcasting platform. Choose a catchy title and create a captivating description that includes a few high searched keywords to draw more attention to your episodes.

You can monetize your podcast the same way you can a blog. You can reach out to businesses to gain direct sponsorships, promote products or services through affiliate marketing, or sell your own products and services. You can transform older content for a membership or subscription option for listeners. Additionally, ask listeners to donate to your podcast by adding a donation option on your website.

Influential Marketing

Influential marketing is another type of affiliate marketing that can bring in hundreds and thousands of dollars. An influencer can use the same commission methods in traditional affiliate marketing—pay per click, pay per lead, and pay per sale. Where influencers make serious money is from campaigns. These tend to be a series of marketing posts where the influencer and brand collaborate. These campaigns can be composed of reviews, unboxings, live video and how-to's, or images showing their brand or product in daily use.

Becoming an influencer is a bit more challenging. You need to have a social presence with a large following. Many companies are seeking out influencers that not only have a huge following but, more importantly, are viewed as an expert or authority figure in their domain. Some influencers have a small following, but their following is incredibly loyal. These influencers are valuable to companies or brands looking to gain traction in a new market or with a different audience than they typically promote to.

TikTok and Instagram are the two social platforms where brands are closely looking for the best influencers. You can take matters into your own hands and reach out to companies that you already love.

There are also influence marketing platforms that allow you to create portfolios, pitch campaign ideas, and begin collaborating with brands seeking out influencers. Most influencer platforms only cater to businesses or brands looking for individuals to collaborate with. There are a select few that allow influencers to create profiles to be viewed by companies for consideration. These include:

- Afluencer
- Upfluence
- ShoutCart (for Instagram influencers)
- Social Bond
- Grapevine (for YouTube, Instagram, and Facebook influencers)
- AspireIQ

Pros and Cons

There are many reasons why creating a passive income from affiliate marketing is appealing, but there are also some drawbacks to be aware of.

One perk of affiliate marketing is you don't have to worry about customer support or supplying the products. The brand or company you get the affiliate link from has to handle all the customer relations. You just need to direct the customers to them. This is also a flexible income. You can work from anywhere, set your own goals for what you want to make. The effort you put in has the biggest impact on what you earn.

The cons are few, and relate more to the outside work you need to generate a substantial income stream. You need to have a platform with a loyal audience base. To attract these followers, you need to implement proper SEO, such as searching for relevant keywords, knowing where to place them, and increasing engagement. This will get your content ranked higher, which increases the number of views and possible clicks the content will attract.

The one set back; to generate a substantial income, you have to put the time into creating valuable content. Whether you are making videos or blog posts, you need to publish engaging, memorable, and valuable content. This is not something everyone has the time to do. While technically, you only have to post content containing the affiliate link once, you need to continuously publish content that keeps your page active.

Chapter 2: Network Marketing

If you love meeting new people and share everything on social media, network marketing is an ideal passive income stream for you. The key to success with this passive income stream is to be your genuine self. Your personality and charisma will attract others to buy and join you on this passive income journey.

What is Network Marketing

Multi-level marketing (MLM) is a network marketing business model where you 'work' for a company selling goods or services. You often build a team of independent sales representatives who sell the same products or assist in closing sales. You make a commission of the products you sell and, depending on the company, you make a bonus from how well the rest of your team does. Some businesses operate on this multi-level tier system, or they may just have you sell products without recruiting. With the combination of a tier system and sale of products, there is potential to make a decent income and how much you make depends on your own effort. With most businesses, those who started early and are at the top of the tier tend to make the most money as they bring in more commissions from their downlines (the people they recruited) and anyone who gets added from the people they add. This is not the case with all network marketing businesses. In some, it does not matter when you get added to someone else's downline; you can outearn the person who recruited you if you build a team of motivated individuals who build a significant team for themselves. If the person who added you only slowly adds more people to their team and does not focus on product sales, you can outearn them.

Beware of Pyramid Schemes

MLMs can be pyramid schemes, but there are characteristics of pyramid schemes that will help you identify which is legitimate and which is not. First, pyramid schemes are often illegal business models. These focus primarily on recruiting individuals and convincing them to pay an upfront cost for a starter kit or pay for training sessions before they can get started. This is how the company makes most of its money. They are not concerned about selling products but only about recruiting more people. Many of the individuals spam everyone they know to get more salespeople under their name. Typical pyramid schemes make it impossible for you to out-earn the person who recruited you.

Finding Reputable Companies

Many reputable MLM companies have single and multi-tier systems. Those with single-tier systems tend to be safer to join, but a few have well-established tier structures that do not limit how much you can make. Some companies you may already be aware of include:

- Avon
- Mary Kay
- Excell Communications
- Tupperware
- Beachbody
- Amway
- Herbalife

It is best to research a company before committing. You want to ensure that the business is encouraging the sales of products and not just recruiting salespeople. Check the history of the company; have they been accused of being a pyramid scheme? Also, consider the products. Are the products you will have to sell ones that you use or foresee yourself using? It will be much easier to promote the products if you are enthusiastic about them.

Generating Income

Most network marketers make a few hundred dollars a month, while others have made six figures a year. Aside from having a highly social personality, creating a steady income from this option does require some innovative business sense. You need to attract people to the products and services you are selling, while also finding individuals who will build their own team from the opportunity. This can involve more of your time, but there are many ways that you can automate some aspects of the process. A few tips to keep in mind:

- Build a team from your customers. If you want to get others to sign up under you, they should already love the product and services themselves. Trying to present a business opportunity to someone who does not know about what they are expected to sell will get you many no's. Focus on selling the products, then keep an eye on the people who naturally talk about what they are using. These people are already doing what needs to be done to build a team of their own, and a majority of that is to share and get others interested.
- Host parties. Take advantage of using technology to your advantage to gather a larger group of people to present the product and service to. Online parties allow you to invite others and them to invite people they know. You can have giveaways and special offers for those who buy.
- Social media marketing is a core component of marketing products. You want your friends and their friends to know what you are offering. Take the time to understand how algorithms work and how you can get your content viewed by a larger number of users.

Pros and Cons

Many companies require some type of investment, either purchasing their products to sell or paying a business fee each month. It can be hard to identify which companies are legitimate for this reason. You must do your research before you sign up as a representative.

You may need to keep your own inventory. So companies require you to purchase a small inventory to sell, which can take up a lot of space in your home. It can also mean getting stuck with a wide range of items that you do not intend on using or can sell.

It is highly competitive, and people have gotten so used to being 'sold' that they often ignore new friend requests or invites. The business you go with can impact how resistant others will be; most people don't mind getting invited to a makeup party or Tupperware show, but sharing weight loss products can get a lot of negative feedback.

Getting started can take a lot of time and effort. Trying to sell and build a team at the same time can become overwhelming. It can also take months before you start earning money; as a general rule, most people need to be presented with an offer a minimum of five times before saying yes. Many people quit before they have even given themselves a chance to build a legitimate income.

Those who have the patience and determination can make five to six figures a year while cutting down on the time they dedicate to their business. Many have found it possible to gradually build their income while only working their business in small pockets of time throughout the day.

Chapter 3: Dropshipping

Dropshipping has been around for many years. It offers individuals a low-cost business model that can bring in big returns. It takes time, and more maintenance is involved, but it can be a highly successful revenue stream. Dropshipping allows you to open your own store without having to handle any physical products yourself. You often set up an online store and find a third-party seller who will then fulfill orders purchased on your online store.

Creating a Market Strategy

Market research is essential for finding products and understanding your target audience. You can search for trending products to include in your store. Ones that are currently selling well are a great starting point. With a bit of searching, you can find products on their way to best selling status. These products get you ahead of competitors and help you take advantage of lower marketing fees. Some resources to make use of to help identify trending products include:

- Kickstarter
- Wish
- Google Trends

Another way to find the right products is to identify a target market. This can help you narrow down your product options while also serving a large enough audience such as dog lovers, nurses, crafters. Take advantage of seasonal trends as well. Narrowing down a niche market can result in less competition, and your marketing efforts will not cost as much since you are targeting a small group of people. It is a good idea to start in a smaller niche. Once you have established a successful store with that market, you can expand to attract new customers that might not initially fall into your niche market.

Look at what your competitors are doing. Do not limit this research to products and prices. You want to try to identify their sales strategy, which can help you uncover products they may add to their stores. You may not be able to add the same products to your ecommerce store at the same price as your competitors. You might want to hold off on adding these items until you have established your store and created your unique brand.

Think outside the box when searching for products. Many people post product-related videos; this can be a way to spot trending products. If a video has had comments, shares, or likes in the past three days, this can be a good candidate product to add to your store. While you are looking for videos on your social sites, do a quick search of the social media shopping platform.

By doing these searches, you gain a substantial list of items you want to begin selling in your store.

Finding Suppliers

You can find wholesalers and manufacturers to stock your online store by using a dropshipping supplier directory. If you already know the product or at least the niche you want to sell, this will take little time to find the right supplier. Some of the best suppliers include (Ferreira, 2021):

- Oberlo
- DropnShop
- Cj Dropshipping
- Supplymedirect
- CROV

To simplify the process, you can set up your ecommerce store with a site that automatically connects you with reputable suppliers.

Creating an Online Store

Shopify is a widely used site that allows individuals to set up an online store and connects shop owners directly with supplies. They have integrated the Oberlo marketplace that helps you find products to sell, which you can import to display in your store. When someone purchases an item from your Shopify store, you just need to ensure all the information is correct on the customer order form. You approve the order, and the product is shipped directly to the customer from the supplier.

Oberlo allows you to track how much inventory a third-party supplier has. When they run out of a particular item that you may offer in your store, you can quickly take action to either remove that item or mark it as temporarily unavailable.

Generating Traffic

Driving traffic to your store is essential to a successful dropshipping business. You can do this in several ways. You can promote products on your social media account and by word of mouth. If you have a blog, YouTube channel, or podcast, you can include ads to your site to attract more customers from your followers.

While you need little money to get started in dropshipping, you will need to spend on marketing to get customers to your store. Many successful dropshippers recommend allocating at least $500 to marketing costs when you first start an ecommerce store (Ferreira, 2021).

Pros and Cons

You do not have to purchase inventory with a dropshipping business. You can set up an ecommerce store with minimal upfront starting costs. You also have a wide range of products you can sell.

There is less risk involved because you don't have to purchase inventory. You won't have to deal with the stress of unloading items that you can't sell. With traditional retail businesses, you often have a stockpile of items that you need to sell. You do not need to worry about products that are not selling. If an item is not selling well, you can remove it from your online store without loss.

There are fewer costs to starting a dropshipping business. Since you do not have to keep a physical inventory, you do not need to invest in a warehouse to store supplies or choose a physical location to sell your item. You also do not have to keep track of inventory. This means you will not have to spend time counting and managing what you sell. Even as your business grows, the cost of operating your dropshipping store remains significantly lower than a brick-and-mortar store.

You can operate a dropshipping business from just about anywhere. All you need to keep your business going is a computer/laptop and quality internet service.

The convenience and flexibility of starting a dropshipping business make it an enticing business venture. While this is great for those wanting to start their own business, this also means it can be highly competitive. With low starting costs and ease of setting up an online store, many people and even companies have dropshipping businesses and sell products at a substantially low price.

Since you are not stocking your own inventory, you have to rely on the third-party seller to have your products available. Almost all third-party sellers supply the same products to other business owners, which means that what they have to provide can change daily. It is not easy to see how much inventory the supplier has, resulting in delays while fulfilling orders.

Shipping costs can become confusing. You can set up your ecommerce store to automatically add shipping costs to a customer's order, making things easy. Unfortunately, with a dropshipping business, you will be working with multiple third-party sellers. A customer can purchase two or more items from your store, and each of these items may come from a different supplier; this means your customer now has two or more different shipping costs. It is not the best idea to pass all these shipping costs onto the customer. You can set up an automatic flat shipping fee, but calculating these can be complex. Setting a price that is too low can result in losing money.

While you don't have to handle any shipping or order fulfillment tasks, you will have to take responsibility for when things do not ship right. If your supplier forgets to include an item you will have to handle the customer service and apologize to the customer. You also do not have much control over packaging. Low-quality packaging can damage products or disappoint buyers.

Along with this lack of control over packing and shipping, there is little room to brand your own business. Many of the products you supply will carry the supplier's branding. If you do want to include your own branding on items, most suppliers will require a minimum order to be placed.

Chapter 4: Selling on Amazon

Amazon is one of the biggest ecommerce stores around, and you can start selling and earning through Amazon a few ways. Many think of selling products as the only option to selling on Amazon, but if you are a creative person, there are even more possibilities.

Fulfillment By Amazon (FBA)

Fulfill by Amazon (FBA) allows you to sell products and keep a stock inventory in Amazon's fulfillment center. Amazon will then ship, pack, and provide customer service for all items you sell. This allows you the perks of having an ecommerce store without having to worry about all these other details.

Setting up a Seller Account

You can have an Individual plan or Professional plan. With an Individual plan, you pay a flat rate each time you sell an item. With a Professional plan, you pay a monthly fee no matter how many or few items you sell. On top of these fees, Amazon also takes a portion of each sale as a 'referral fee'. This fee will fluctuate depending on the category the time is sold under.

You can sell on Amazon by reselling items, manufacturing your own product/brand to sell, or if you have a Shopify account, you can link your products to be sold on Amazon. There are restrictions to what you can sell, however. The product, category, and brand may impact whether you can sell a particular item or not. Some products are prohibited for sale, others may require special permission to list, and a few do not allow for third-party selling.

You can use a business email to start a new Amazon seller account or your current Amazon customer account to sign up. The items you plan to sell may determine which account you want to set up. To create a seller account, you will need:

- Active credit card
- Government ID
- Tax information
- Phone number
- Bank account

Pros and Cons

You can stay up-to-date with your seller account via the Amazon Seller app. The app makes it even more convenient to establish a profitable side business. With the app, you can track your sales, fulfill orders, find additional items to sell, update and edit product images, and add new items to sell.

After the initial time spent searching for and listing products, the business is relatively easy to maintain. Most profitable sellers on Amazon spend between 5 to 20 hours maintaining their business each week. On average, a third of new sellers have seen profits of over $4,000 within the first three months and have seen this income grow, reaching five figures within the first one or two years (Connolly, 2021).

You do need to invest money and time. Many sellers saw success investing around $500 into their Amazon business, and saw more success with getting their products listed than others who spent well over that amount (Connolly, 2021). The biggest issue is that you need to spend time researching products and creating listings at first. Product research is crucial to success.

EBook Publishing

If you have a knack for writing, publishing books online can lead to a hefty passive income. This is truly a passive income stream because once you do the initial work of writing and designing a book, there is little maintenance needed afterward. This is not to say that publishing just one book will generate $10,000, but publishing multiple high-quality books does have the potential to make you money for years. This is ideal for monetizing the content on other platforms for those who already have blogs, YouTube channels, or podcasts.

There are also multiple avenues to publish electronically, including Amazon Kindle Direct Publishing, Kobo, Smashwords, and Draft2Digital. These platforms each have their own benefits and drawbacks. For example, if you publish with Amazon, you get higher royalties, but they retain exclusive distribution. Smashwords, Kobo, and Draft2Digital have lower royalties, but allow you to distribute through other platforms and avenues. This means that your profit per unit may be a tad smaller, but your overall possible sales is higher. You also may wish to consider what markets are most important to you. Amazon is the biggest player in the American market, but Kobo holds a large chunk of sales in Canada and Europe.

Doing a little research will help you identify the best niche to focus on. Some of the best selling eBooks fall into the following categories:

- Business/Investing
- Computer and tech
- Health, fitness, and dieting
- Self-help
- Parenting and relationships

Before you begin to jump into the writing process, you want to ensure there is an audience for the book you write. You can do a quick search for books that may be similar to yours already for sale on Amazon. To find out what books are selling best on Kindle, you can search the "Amazon Kindle eBooks Best Sellers and More" category. You can do the same with Kobo and Apple Books by searching your intended category. It will automatically sort by bestseller. This also helps you identify your competitors. Reading the reviews of bestseller books will give you an advantage of what to include or not include in your own books.

Once you have taken the time to search for similar titles, you want to learn if there is a big enough audience buying these books. Using the same process as mentioned previously, search for your book's category under "Amazon Kindle eBooks Best Sellers and More." Click on the books that are the most similar to your idea and look under the product details. You will see the Amazon Best Sellers Rank; the number next to this is the most important. If the book has a number below 1,000, it has a high number of sales, but it also means that it's a very competitive title. If the book has a number between 1,000 to 30,000, it has done well selling copies, and there is less competition. If the book ranks above 30,000, the sales are not great, but there is also very little competition. The sweet spot is that middle range (1,000 to 30,000). With these rankings, you can feel more confident that your book will do well in this category, and there is less competition to fight against to get higher sales.

Once you have taken these first two steps, you want to honestly evaluate how your book idea will fare against the top of this category. When you first launch your book, breaking the top three in your category will ensure your books get plenty of exposure. They are listed first in the New Release section.

Professional Tips

Title — The title is the most important component of your book. You can write the best content there is, but it won't make you any money if you have a bad title. Your title needs a main title and a subtitle. The main title needs to capture potential readers' attention. It needs to be memorable while also hinting at the book's topic. The subtitle should explain how the book will help the reader. Consider what problem the book solves and how their life will change once they finish the book. A subtitle that covers these key points will intrigue the audience. To draw in more attention, use sensory words in your subtitle that will help it stand out, such as:

- Vibrant
- Delicious

- Nutritious
- Cringeworthy
- Monotonous

Cover Design — After the title, the cover design is the most crucial aspect of your book. The cover is the first impression audiences get of the content and quality of the book. A poor cover design will get overlooked every time. Successful cover designs contain two crucial components:

1. The title is clear and easy to read. Potential readers will see just a thumbnail of your book design first, and they need to be able to read the title from this thumbnail. You need to use the right typeface and font size to ensure that your title is clear and legible, even on a smaller scale.
2. It uses bold colors, an exciting image, or a careful balance of both. The cover design needs to stand out and capture the audience's attention immediately.

You can certainly attempt to create your own cover design if you have design experience. It is much better to hire a professional to create one for you. Sites like Fiverr can match you with a professional designer to create a gorgeous cover with very little investment. Be sure to look through samples of the individual's work before hiring them. Other places you can try for professional cover designs include:

- Upwork
- Happy Self Publishing
- 99 Designs
- BookBaby
- EBook Launch
- Deviant Art

The prices and packages offered with the above option will vary, but is well worth the cost, considering an amazing cover design is key to generating higher sales.

Description — The first thing customers are going to read from you is the description of the book. The description needs to sell your book; it needs to be compelling and persuade customers to buy what you have written. Your description should summarize key points of your book that benefit the reader. There should be bullet points that touch on the problems the book will solve without giving away how it solves the problem. To write a persuasive book description that will get customers to buy, consider the following tips:

1. The first sentence of the description is the most essential component. It needs to hook the reader by telling them what problem your book will solve for them.
2. Add one or two "what if" statements to get the reader to imagine what their life would be like once their problem is solved. Does the information allow them more free time, money, productivity, better relationships? Tap into the readers' pain points and help them envision a better life because of the solution they will find in the pages of your book.
3. Show your authority. Even if you don't have a degree or best-selling credentials, there are ways you can tell your reader they can trust you as an authority figure. How has the information helped you transform your life?
4. Don't ask them to take action; tell them. When writing their book description, many make a huge mistake by asking the reader to buy, when they should simply say, "Get your copy today."

Marketing — Before you launch your book, you need to have a solid plan to generate hype around your book. Have a list of people who will read and write reviews; they should also promote your book on their social media accounts. Let these individuals know that you are giving them an advanced copy of the book and when they should write the review. If you can come up with a list of 50 people, you should garner about 25 reviews by the time you launch. This gets your book ranking higher when it first launches.

Next, you want to start dropping hints about your book on your social media accounts. This builds anticipation around the launch. If you have a blog, you want to start dropping hints to your readers and mention the launch to your email list. You don't want to start pushing sales; just bring awareness to the launch.

Around two to four weeks before you launch your book, it's a good idea to send out free samples to those on your mailing list. This can be the introduction to the book or a snippet of one of the chapters.

Publish your book on your preferred platform a week before the launch date. This gives the people you sent an advanced copy time to write their reviews. If you get at least 10 reviews, you can take advantage of using book promotion sites. These early views can end up giving you a massive boost in early sales.

Pricing — There are four options when choosing the right price point to start selling your book at. You can increase or decrease the price at any time. Each time your book sells, you get a percentage of royalty fees. These are broken down as follows:

- You will get 35% of the royalty for books priced between $.99 to $2.98.
- You get 70% of royalty fees for books priced between $2.99 to $9.99.
- You get 35% of royalty fees for books priced at $10.00 and above.
- If you enroll your book in Amazon's Kindle Unlimited program, you get a percentage based on the number of pages read each month.

Many people automatically gravitate to pricing their book between $2.99 and $9.99 because they receive the highest royalties at this price point. This can be a huge mistake when you first launch your book. At the launch of your book, you want to generate the most sales; pricing your book at just $.99 can help accomplish this. The more sales you get at the start of your launch, the higher your ranking will be. It does not matter that your book is only $.99; what matters is that it is selling.

Starting with a low price has additional benefits. You can use this as an incentive for readers who have not purchased yet to get their copy before the price goes up. This also helps you get your book featured on promotional book sites like Book Bub and BookSends. These sites will promote your book while it is either available for free or $.99. Keep in mind, many of the sites require a subscription fee, but the fee is worth it to gain sales outside of Amazon. When individuals from these sites purchase your book, Amazon recognizes this and views your book as profitable. Amazon will then promote your book for free.

Promotions — Kindle Unlimited and Kobo allow you to set up promotion days where your book is offered at a discount or for free. This can be a great way to generate sales during the first two to three days of the launch and months after the launch. When it comes to generating a steady stream from publishing on your platform, you need to promote your book continuously. This will remind readers who have not purchased the book that is still available and inform new readers that you have published a book. You can entice more people to buy your book before you increase the price. When increasing the price, do it in increments to take advantage of a boost in sales.

Pros and Cons

Publishing your books is entirely free. There are no upfront costs or listing fees you need to worry about. This makes getting started easy, and there is no risk of losing money with this business venture.

Writing a book is not as easy as it appears. You need to spend time writing quality content, edit it thoroughly, and have an eye-catching cover design. On top of this, you need a marketing strategy. As nice as it would be to publish a book and let the money roll in, that doesn't happen. While you won't need to spend money on getting your books published, it takes a considerable amount of time to publish a successful book.

Anyone can write a book and publish it, but if you want to make money, you need to take the time to properly market, promote, and create the content. It can take months to complete a book, and if you do not have an email list, it can be hard to get enough people interested in purchasing your book.

Low-Content Books

If writing a full eBook sounds like too much work or you don't have the time to commit to a big project like a complete manuscript, you can still take advantage of publishing on Amazon with low-content books. Think journals, coloring books, trackers, calendars. These books require minimal writing on your part. You still use Kindle Direct Publish, but you use their print-on-demand feature with published paperback books.

Ideas

You can find low-content books just about anywhere. These include:

- Blank journals
- Prompted journals
- Habit trackers (food, exercise, meditation, gratitude)
- Activity books
- Coloring books
- Recipe books
- Guest books (for wedding, birthday, anniversaries)

You can create one template for a lined journal, change the cover design, and have an unlimited number of low-content books for sale in a short time. You can also create a blank-lined journal with a simple heading at the top of the page, for example: "Today I am grateful for…" These journals are just one of the many ways you can create a book with the same interior and use it repeatedly.

Unlike the cover for eBooks, the cover design for these low-content books can be just about anything. Use a simple image and change the background cover, add a famous inspiration quote, create a pattern, or just add a bunch of different shapes. You can make these covers using popular websites like Canva. If you are publishing an eBook, these low-content books can be a great addition that allows you to bundle the two together and increase your profits.

You can also do this with products you may have up for sale, though this does take some out-of-the-box thinking. For example, if you are selling sheets or coffee mugs, create a gratitude journal and encourage buyers to relax under their sheets or with a cup of coffee while counting their blessings for the day. If you are selling bakeware, include a blank recipe book where buyers can keep their favorite recipes.

Creating Low-Content Books

First, decide the size of your book: 6X9 in., 8x10 in., or 8.5x 11 in. Keep in mind, you can also make your low-content book available as a digital download, and the standard size for these types of printable is 8.5X11 in.

Decide if the content in your book will go all the way to the edges or to stop centered on the page. If you plan to have designs on the interior of your book, you might want these to spill over to the edge of the page. In this case, you would like to choose bleed on. The no bleed option will frame your design with a white border. Decide this early on; with bleed on you need to add .125 in. to the width of your book and .24 in. to the height. For example, if you are going with an 8.5X11 trim, you need to adjust it to 8.625X11.25 in.

Adding color to the interior of your books increases the price you need to sell them at. This may seem like an appealing idea because a higher price means bigger profits but consider that many of the best selling low-content books are typically priced around seven to nine dollars. These books tend to bring in a profit of just three dollars, and you also benefit from using the expanded distribution feature. When you add color to the exterior, this can bump up your sale price to over $13.00, and you would not receive any royalties per sale. To obtain the same profits, you would need to increase your price to over $18.00, and at this price point, you would not be able to use expanded distribution. To use expanded distribution, you would need to sell your low-content book for at least $20.00. At this price, your book will most likely not sell. While the color interior will make your designs look nicer, going with grayscale will improve your chances of making a profit.

With these in mind, you can create your low-content books, as mentioned using Canva for the cover design. You can also use:

- Google Slides
- PowerPoint
- Microsoft Word
- InDesign

You can use these programs to design the cover and lined pages for the interior. You will need to add the lines to your pages; Amazon will not automatically print your books with lined pages. This is easily done by adding a table to a blank page with your desired number of rows, usually around 24. Once you have your table added, delete the outside borders, which will leave only the lines on the page. When you have this done for one page, duplicate the page for how many pages you want your finished journal to have, for example, 100 pages.

Not all books need lined pages. You can promote your low-content book as a sketch pad, in which case you will still need to use one of these programs to create your book, but you will just create a document that contains the blank pages.

This process can be made even simpler by signing up for a site that helps you design low-content books from start to finish for a low monthly fee, such as Book Bolt and Interior Builder. These will streamline the process and tend to cost under $10 a month.

Pros and Cons

With this option, you can quickly get a wider variety of books published, and you do not have to worry about keeping an inventory. There are no upfront investments you need to make either.

It does take some time to get the correct formatting and learning how to keyword your books, so they get found easily, other than that, there is no additional investment needed. With the ability to use the same interior designs for multiple books, you don't have to create each book from beginning to end.

The only con with this option is it can be a highly competitive category to generate sales in. With the right keyword, you can get your book noticed. Target specific audiences, such as dog lovers for books that feature a dog on them. This option is best to sell many different designs to increase the chances of making a substantial profit.

Chapter 5: Digital Goods

We are not referring to just eBooks and courses. There are many ways you can create digital products that generate a steady stream of income. Vector art is one of the most popular forms of digital goods. These can be sold on many design sites like Canva or even Design Space (a cutting machine program for Cricut users). As you will learn, you can find many ways to create digital products and enjoy a steady income stream from very little time or financial investments.

Printables

Many printables can mimic low-content books. You do not need to worry about the printing cost for printing in color; you can make these stand out with lots of colors and details. You will not need to add blank pages for printables. Instead, you can create a full-page layout that the customer can then download and print as many as they need. Printables can include a wide range of items such as:

- Habit trackers
- Calendars
- Social media templates
- Checklists
- Coloring pages
- Worksheets
- Schedules
- Games

These can be easily created using Canva. You can sell each page individually or create a bundle to sell multiple templates together. Printables can be sold through your own website or you can make an Etsy shop. Creative Market is another site that will allow you to sell printables.

Apps

You do not need coding experience to create an app. Online services like BuildFire helps create mobile apps for you or through one of their templates. Apps can generate income through in-app ads, affiliate links, or by charging a download fee. Besides having to do minor updates or adding new features once you have your app created, there is little time spent maintaining this income stream. If you have a blog, you can create an app that provides readers instant access to specific content. For example, if you blog about cooking, you can create a recipe app.

Photography/Video Presets

Photo and video presets are used by everyone. These add special lighting, effects, colors, and more to images and videos. Thanks to social media, these have become high demand. Filters, stickers, and themes can be created and sold through your website or places like Creative Market, FilterGrade, and Behance. You can create presets using popular video and photo software like Adobe Lightroom and Premiere, Final Cut Pro, and DaVinci.

If you have any of these editing programs, you can create a preset package that can build you a sizable side income. Making minor adjustments to the presets you create can offer a wider selection for users and requires little time. When you sell your presets, you want to give users a view of how the presets will affect their images. Creating before and after photos will help users see what they are getting. You can use your social media accounts to start marketing and promote your presets using them on the images and videos you share.

Photography

Stock photography is always in demand. If you have any photography skills, there are plenty of stock photo websites you can sell your images to. Stock photos are used for blogs, advertising, and much more.

You do not need to have an expensive camera. Many people have been able to use their smartphones to take a variety of stock photos. You can also set up a subscription service that allows people to use the images you take for a small monthly fee. The most popular stock photography sites are Adobe Stock, iStock, Shutterstock, and Getty Images.

While this is a passive income, those who create a steady income are constantly adding to their online gallery. Many stock sites have specific requirements images need to meet before making them available on their sites.

Setting Up an Ecommerce

You can set up a digital store and begin uploading your products quickly. The most popular sites include:

- Etsy
- Shopify
- Facebook
- Personal/Business Blog (Woocommerce)
- BigCommerce

Many of these charge a small listing fee for each product you list. Having a solid description of the product is essential. Use keywords that describe your product and terms people are using when searching for similar products. This will get your item found more quickly, even when just starting.

Chapter 6: Trading and Investing

Many shy away from investing and trading as a passive income because it can be a complex process if you don't know where to start. Learn how to get into trading and investing to put away more for retirement, vacations, or add to your current income. Trading and investing can be as passive or active as you desire. Those who are more involved can make a substantial amount of money daily. A more passive approach may take longer to build up, but requires less effort. Keep in mind; there is always a risk when it comes to trading and investing. A general rule with this passive income is never to invest money that you do not intend to lose.

Real Estate Investments Trusts

Real estate investment trusts (REIT) allow you to make money from real estate without owning property or handling the maintenance and additional tenant complaints from owning a physical piece of property. You can invest in apartment complexes, facilities, hotels, retail centers, and many other commercial properties with REITs. You then get paid a dividend on your investment and these can be traded just like any traditional stock. REITs fall into three categories:

- Equity - These are the most common and largest categories. Equity REITs are properties where the income is generated through rental payments.
- Mortgage - Mortgage REITs generate income through a net interest margin because they are loans or mortgage agreements.
- Hybrid - Hybrid REITs have components of both equity and mortgage REITs. There is income-producing property and loans or mortgage agreements on those properties that bring in a stream of income for both avenues.

To get started, you can begin to invest as little as $500; sites like Realty Mogul, Fundrise, and Steitwise allow you to invest in real estate quickly and easily.

REITs offer a long-term income stream. They can be easy to buy and trade, but you will want to do your research before deciding which REIT to buy into. REITs are registered with the Securities and Exchange Commission (SEC). You can verify this by searching the SECs EDGAR system, which will also provide you with annual and quarterly reports of available REITs (Chen, 2020).

Keep in mind that any money you make from a REIT investment will be taxed as a regular income. REITs can also have high transaction fees.

Exchange-Traded Funds

Exchange-traded funds (ETF) offer the best of stock trading and mutual funds. These funds allow you to buy and sell a bundle of assets throughout the trading day. They often have lower fees, and many carry lower risks. Instead of investing in a single stock, you are investing in a more diversified basket of stocks. For example, SPY is a bundle of stocks that follow the S&P 500, HACK is a bundle of cyber security funds, and FONE has a bundle of options that focus on smartphone funds (Voigt, 2021).

ETFs are a standard option for many online brokers. The most common types include (Voigt, 2021):

- Stock ETFs are less risky and are ideal for long-term returns.
- Commodity ETFs are related to raw goods such as coffee or oil. These funds can vary greatly, and you want to know where you are investing in the physical stockpile of the item or companies that produce the product. These funds can have higher risk levels and are subject to different tax regulations.

- Bond ETFs are low-risk investments that do not have a maturity date like traditional bonds. These generate regular cash payments.
- International ETFs focus on foreign investments, which can include investing in an individual country or country blocs.
- Sector ETFs allow you to invest in companies in one of the eleven stock market sectors. These include health care, industrial, and financial sectors. These carry less risk than investing in a single company that falls into one of these sectors. You can track specific business cycles and make a well-rounded judgment of which sector is best to invest in.

Dividend Stocks

Dividend stocks are investments in a company that allow you to reap the benefits from a company's profits. Payments are made on a monthly, quarterly, or yearly schedule. You can use this payout to reinvest and buy more shares of that company. Investing in dividend stocks can be done through many online brokerages without the need for a financial advisor.

There are a few restrictions that may apply to dividend stocks. Some companies only allow you to buy shares of the company if you are an employee or already own the stock. There are limitations to how you can buy or sell your company's shares, reducing the freedom you have with this investment.

When looking for dividend stocks to invest in, consider the following:

- Look at the company's return on equity. This number gives you an estimate of the company's net income and how much dividends are paid out to shareholders.

- How much debt does the company have? A company with a high debt-to-equity ratio will have to spend more money paying off these debts and less going to shareholders.
- Does the company have a steady and increasing profit margin? A company with a growing profit margin over the years will be in a good financial position to pay out dividends, while a decreasing profit margin will struggle to pay investors.
- Choose companies that have been publicly traded for at least 10 years.
- Find undervalued stocks. These are companies selling at lower than they are worth, meaning you can buy into them at a low rate and reap the rewards later. Undervalued stocks are due to the market overreacting, which can be a good time to invest.

Dividend stocks are genuinely passive income. Aside from monitoring how your stock is doing, once you have invested in the stock, there is not much else you need to do. If you set up a dividend reinvestment plan (DRIP), earnings are automatically reinvested into that company.

While this is a highly appealing investment opportunity that can benefit you long-term, there are no guarantees when investing. A company may go out of business or completely stop paying dividends at any time.

Chapter 7: Rent Your Space

Having a rental property has been the most common steady income stream for a long time. Although this is still a favorable income opportunity, owning an apartment or secondary home to rent is not the most financially suitable way to take advantage of rental spaces. Even renting out a spare bedroom and taking in a roommate does not always result in the best situations. Thanks to rental sites like Airbnb, it has become easier to rent out your spare rooms for a short period.

Rental Property

Rental properties have been a long-time safer option for creating a passive income. These, however, require a substantial upfront investment. Even if you have the money to purchase a rental property, you also need to consider the maintenance and emergency expenses. You can get an estimate of these maintenance fees by calculating one percent of the property value (Dillon, 2018). Consider also that you might not always have the most responsible tenants, which can cost you thousands of dollars and added stress.

If you already own a rental property, renting out rooms instead of the entire property can bring you in a little extra income for no more effort. For example, if you have a single-family three-bedroom home that you typically rent out to one family for $1500 a month, you can rent each room to different tenants for $600 to $700 a month. You would bring in an additional $300 to $600 a month. Each tenant would be responsible for their own portion of the rent and would have their personal space with the ability to share common spaces like the living room, kitchen, bathrooms, and outdoor areas.

Renting Your Spare Room

Listing your room for rent on sites like Airbnb has its pros and cons as well. You get your listing exposed to a wide range of travelers. You only have to worry about blocking out certain days when guests will be staying there. For the most part, those who use these services understand that it is your home, and are more respectful of the space. This is not for every person, but it is a general rule. The other nice thing about renting space on Airbnb is that the people looking for a room to stay in, are typically not going to be there the entire time. Many people are just looking for a place to sleep that is cheaper than most hotel rooms.

There are additional perks to offering your spare room for rent on Airbnb. If you become a Superhost, you can get extra freebies. A Superhost has phenomenal reviews and meets other requirements, like hosting for at least a year, quick response time, and one cancellation for every 100 booked. Many companies offer hosts free samples, from toiletries to mattresses, sheets, and pillows. On top of this, you can get a $100 freebie bonus from Airbnb.

Choosing the right price for your listing can be done in a few ways. First, decide how many days you are willing to rent your spare space, then determine your monthly fees if you were just renting out this room to a traditional tenant. Divide your monthly expenses by the days you are willing to rent out your room, and you will get an estimate of how much you want to rent your space for. If, however, you only want to rent your area a few times a month, this will give you a high price that will not get your space rented out. Instead, look at what similar listings are charging, then divide your total expense by 30. This will give you the minimum you want to charge per night, whether you are only renting for a few days each month or most of the month. Also, consider that you will need to clean the space after each guest. You can add cleaning fees in addition to the nightly fees. This helps cover the cost of cleaning materials, laundry, and the time you need to spend doing the cleaning.

This is a good option for those who have a spare room that is not being used. All you need to do is take quality images of your space and get it listed on Airbnb. Then you just have to worry about the cleaning and staying up to date with bookings, such as messaging potential guests and verifying their identity. Though this can be a passive income, there is no guarantee that you will be booked as much as you would like. This means you can't always be sure how much you will earn in a month, especially at the beginning.

Conclusion

It doesn't matter what age you are; whether you just graduated college or are nearing retirement, a passive income is essential. The right passive income can complement your current earnings or replace them. It gives you financial security for the future and allows you to explore entrepreneurship without most of the major risks.

This book has provided you with various passive income options and easy to get started steps. You have learned the pros and cons of each possibility to decide which one works with your current lifestyle. You can use these suggestions to build a more complex stream of income if you choose. A passive income often begins as a hobby that stems from a passion. This passion drives many people to establish a profitable business where they have more control over their earnings and the hours they work.

A passive income is easy to get started on; though the beginning may take slightly more time to begin seeing a steady income, it is well worth it. You can begin to generate an income in your spare time while working a full-time job or taking care of the kids. Now that you know how, all you need to do is take action and get started!

If you enjoyed this book in anyway, an honest review is always appreciated!

References

Awosika, A. (2021, April 22). *How to make money with Kindle Direct Publishing [case study].* Smart Blogger.
https://smartblogger.com/kindle-publishing/

Brown, A. G. (2018, March 27). *How to make and sell your own Lightroom presets.* Format.
https://www.format.com/magazine/resources/photography/how-to-make-and-sell-lightroom-presets

Chen, J. (2020, June 30). *Owning property via a real estate investment trust.* Investopedia. https://www.investopedia.com/terms/r/reit.asp

Connolly, A. (2021, January 17). *How much money do Amazon sellers make?* Jungle Scout. https://www.junglescout.com/blog/how-much-money-amazon-sellers-make/

Darko. (2020, February 19). *19 amazing MLM statistics you should read in 2020.* Jobs In Marketing. https://jobsinmarketing.io/blog/mlm-statistics/

Dillon, M. (2018, June 23). *How much should a landlord allocate for monthly maintenance & repairs.* SFGate.
https://homeguides.sfgate.com/much-should-landlord-allocate-monthly-maintenance-repairs-80019.html

Enfroy, A. (n.d.). *Affiliate marketing in 2020: what it is and how beginners can start.* The BigCommerce Blog.
https://www.bigcommerce.com/blog/affiliate-marketing/#how-do-affiliate-marketers-get-paid

Ferreira, C. (2021a, January 1). *How to find and work with reliable dropshipping suppliers.* Shopify.
https://www.shopify.com/blog/dropshipping-suppliers

Ferreira, C. (2021b, January 2). *how to start a dropshipping business: A complete playbook for 2021.* Shopify.

https://www.shopify.com/blog/how-to-start-
dropshipping#:~:text=How%20much%20can%20you%20make

Hayes, A. (2021, March 16). *Network marketing.* Investopedia.
https://www.investopedia.com/terms/n/network-marketing.asp

Kevin. (2021, January 11). *Making money with Airbnb in 2021: Why I
rent out our guest room.* Financial Panther.
https://financialpanther.com/making-money-airbnb-rent-guest-
room/

Lake, R. (2019, October 27). *Make money with affiliate marketing.*
Investopedia. https://www.investopedia.com/personal-
finance/affiliate-marketing-can-you-really-make-
money/#:~:text=According%20to%20the%20survey%2C%209

Patel, N. (n.d.). *How to start a blog that generates $3817 a month.* Neil
Patel. https://neilpatel.com/how-to-start-a-blog/#step-10

Roach, A. (2021, March 19). *How to find the perfect dropshipping
products.* Oberlo Dropshipping app.
https://www.oberlo.com/blog/find-perfect-dropshipping-products

Sheehan, A. (2019, March 14). *How much to charge for your Airbnb
rental.* Money under 30. https://www.moneyunder30.com/how-
much-to-charge-for-airbnb

Thackston, K. (2020, February 22). *The power & profits of low-
content Amazon self-publishing (no inventory!).* Marketing Words.
https://www.marketingwords.com/blog/amazon-self-publishing/

Voigt, K. (2021, April 26). *What is an etf? a beginner's complete guide.*
NerdWallet. https://www.nerdwallet.com/article/investing/what-
is-an-etf

WPBeginner Editorial Staff. (2020, January 2). *How to start a podcast (and make it successful) in 2020.* WPBeginner. https://www.wpbeginner.com/wp-tutorials/step-by-step-guide-how-to-start-a-podcast-with-wordpress/

www.ingramcontent.com/pod-product-compliance
Lightning Source LLC
Chambersburg PA
CBHW020758220326
41597CB00012BA/582